For when you're feeling uninspired,
and you don't know how you'll make it thr⟨
This book found you for a reason;
these poems were meant for you.
For the days your soul is heavy
and the world is wearing thin.
I hope these words bring some comfort,
as you read and they settle within.
For when you need a pick-me-up,
if happiness is just out of sight.
You'll find your sunshine soon,
just keep looking for the light.

Things I want to tell you right now:
That I know you'll survive this, even if you don't know how.
There are so many days you've yet to squeeze tight,
there will be more love and sunshine and dazzling light.
I know right now you're enveloped by darkness,
but there are people who love the bones of you regardless
of whether you're at your best or your very worst,
people who would do anything to take away this hurt.
I want you to know that time doesn't always heal,
that you can never take away what you feel,
but you'll learn to live with it, and you'll be okay.
I promise you, there will be better days.

Sometimes you just feel heavy
and it's not apparent why,
like slate grey clouds filling with rain,
putting pressure on the sky.
It's a dark, ugly blanket
covering over your face,
You feel weighed down by emotion,
like you're taking up too much space.
We know the ins and outs of that feeling,
it strikes us all from time to time.
Without feeling heavy you wouldn't notice
when the weight is lifted from your spine
and lightness starts to flow through you.
You no longer feel that weight.
Perhaps we all have to feel heavy sometimes,
to appreciate our true state.

I hope one day when you look at yourself
you see more than skin and bone,
that you don't linger on your cellulite,
and wince at an extra stone,
zooming in on those imperfections
so you can never forget they're there,
the birthmark on your stomach,
and that annoying single grey hair.
I hope soon you can move past
covering up your scars,
because treating yourself like this every day
is like living behind bars.
One day you'll look over
and see that everything about you shines;
that light radiates from within you
and gold runs down your spine.
You won't dodge the full-length mirrors
when you're walking through a city.
Your heart won't drop when you steal a glance,
your eyes won't fill with tears and pity.
Soon you're going to wake up
and see that you've been worthy all along.
Your body is just the instrument,
but your soul is playing the song.

In these days filled with hurt and undeniable sadness,
it's so easy to get caught up in the chorus of madness.
To wrap ourselves up in the stories we hear,
to turn on the news and just want to disappear.
When you look outside the window, there's a whirlwind of sorrow,
but when today has been bleak you must have hope for tomorrow.
It can't rain forever and the sun always rises;
life has a strange way of working out and throwing us surprises.
There's a whole planet out there and we are so small,
so many times I question whether I make any difference at all.
But if seven billion people all questioned themselves that way,
imagine the difference we could all make every day.
Just be a little kinder as we stumble through
this craziness we call life, because we all feel alone.
It's important to know that we're never on our own.
We all have so much more in common than what sets us apart,
just please try to be kind with every ounce of your heart.

I am an extra in so many stories,
just a momentary blurred face,
appearing for a few seconds,
on my way to another place.
I sip tea in the windows of coffee shops
and smile as people walk past,
but they never remember,
they're moving much too fast.
We're always in the background,
all going our separate ways,
tiny fragments of history
as we go about our days.
It's somehow both incredible and a pity,
beautifully bittersweet,
how we're constantly crossing paths with each other,
and yet we never meet.

It's the people who will be there
when it's 2am and cold,
who will sit with you in the morning
and give you a hand to hold,
who don't care what you look like,
because you're more than just skin.
They look past your appearance
and see the person within;
the person who is messy,
who is reckless, sometimes rough,
but none of those things matter,
they're still always there when it's tough.
They are there for the days
when you simply radiate light,
but remain unafraid of the brewing storm;
they never run when others might,
people who put beauty in monotony
and have endless love to spare.
Even when you're miles apart in distance,
you just always know they're there.

If the universe feels heavy
as it weighs down on your shoulders
and you cannot help but fear that the world
is growing colder,
even if your load is frightening,
you don't have to face it all.
I know the world is overwhelming
and right now, you're feeling small.
In this moment you can't see it
but just hold on tonight.
Take it second by second.
Things are going to be alright.

You feel so terribly tiny
when you look up at the moon.
I know you think you're the only one,
but you'll meet that person soon.
There's someone out there, somewhere,
and they too gaze out at the stars.
Deep down, they know you're watching,
no matter how far away they are.
Although you feel alone now,
other people feel that way too.
They're staring into the universe,
and dreaming of the day they'll meet you.

Snapped crayons in an art set
still manage to colour just fine.
Think about glow sticks,
they have to break before they shine,
and how a broken biscuit
still always tastes the same.
You wouldn't throw away a piece
that was missing from a game.
Just because you're not perfect,
doesn't mean you're broken in two.
You're more strong and worthy than ever,
after everything you've been through.

Even when you feel like there's nothing left
and your life is in disarray,
you will always have the knowledge
that the sun will rise and set each day.
There will always be the moonlight
to gaze at and remember your dreams,
and you will forever have the ocean,
even when the world's not what it seems.
You will always have yourself,
you're strong and proud and free.
You are the most important person in your life,
you can be whoever you want to be.

You are more than a number
that appears on a scale.
You are more than a grade,
a pass or a fail.
You are more than a weight,
and what you choose to eat.
You are more than the assumptions
of the people you meet.
You are more than all of these things,
and one day you'll realise
that the only thing that defines you
is what you hold inside.

How often do you look at someone's hair,
and it's beautiful and bold, but you don't want to stare.
You admire someone's resilience, how they have no fear,
but you haven't spoken to them for a year.
It might be weird, to point out how seeing their smile
fills your heart with enough warmth to last a while.
The man singing in the street, with a voice like honey,
those people in your life that make the darkest days feel sunny.
We are all ruled by this silent fear,
when in reality we have no idea
how much that smile or kind word might mean
because people aren't always what they seem.
A painted-on smile might be a mask for sadness,
and we all need to feel loved in this world full of madness.
A compliment could change someone's day,
a lifeline for someone who doesn't want to stay.
How many times a day do you keep those thoughts inside,
so they wait and linger and try to hide?
We push our kind thoughts to the back of our minds,
we'll tell them another day, it's fine,
but why do we leave beautiful words unsaid,
when we could wrap them around someone's heart instead?

When you make your own sunshine,
you can carry it anywhere.
You can keep it in your pocket,
or sprinkle some in your hair.
You can keep it to yourself,
or share it with a friend.
But no matter how much you use,
your supply will never end.
It doesn't matter if it's pouring,
and your umbrella is inside out.
When you keep your sunshine in a bottle,
you will never go without.
Even if the world is gloomy,
and the sky is dark and grey,
you will always have some sunshine,
to brighten up your day.
You can drag the jar behind you
and leave a sunshine trail,
so other people can pick some up
when they are feeling frail.
You don't have to be a superhero,
you can be tall, small, big or thin,
and the recipe is different for everyone,
because sunshine comes from within.

You act like a wallflower,
taking up so little space,
pressed up against the wall like paper,
and no one can see your face.
But no matter how small you think you are,
your impact on people is real.
You don't just fade into the background,
though that's often how you feel.
Because of you someone smiles,
when they think of a certain day.
Someone doesn't like a song,
but they'll listen to it anyway,
because it reminds them of you,
and the warmth you always bring.
One night you gave someone the confidence
to let go and dance and sing.
Because of the way you've touched the world,
it will always remember your name.
Stop trying to be invisible,
and stop trying to be the same.

The things that speak volumes,
about who you really are,
are not how much money you have,
or a house, or a car.
The things that really matter
are the things we hold inside.
Those moments you're truly yourself,
when you open your heart wide.
It's not about a quantity,
having too much or not enough.
Because when it comes down to it,
you are so much more than stuff.

I get lost in the blur of faces in the street,
I fall deep into the eyes of the people I meet.
I can't live on the surface, I have to dive deep
and think of those people, their stories I keep.
I can't let go of the man wearing grey,
his expression matched the colourless sky that day,
and the hardened bus driver with eyes like steel,
perhaps his life has taught him how not to feel.
The girl in the shop operating the till,
animated and bright but sat perfectly still,
who served the lady in the anorak with a stick and loose change,
blessing everyone in sight, which must have seemed strange
to the boy in the hoodie buying pocket money sweets
cheeks flushed bright red, looking down at his feet.
Hundreds of faces everywhere I go,
intricate webs of lives that I will never know.

You're an over-thinker
and you're full up with worry.
You've lost count of how many times
you say that you're sorry.
You're sensitive and soft,
but that doesn't make you weak.
You sense those subtle changes,
in the way that people speak.
When their eye twitches a little,
there's a strange shift in their mood,
and you know that something's wrong,
you can't dismiss as being rude.
You care for people with a fierceness
that you cannot explain.
You are so full of empathy
that you often feel their pain.
Sensitivity was always
perceived as something bad,
a weakness to be hidden,
to wish you never had.
But it's the biggest part of you,
it shows in the things you do and say.
Being an empath is a gift,
and it's beautiful being this way.

There's a magic in this world that isn't hard to find.
It's everywhere you look and it's called... being kind!
It's sewn into the lining of the dress you give to a friend.
It wraps itself around the broken heart you try to mend.
You'll find it when you make your mum a hot cup of tea,
or when you're crouching on the pavement,
saving an injured bumblebee.
It lives inside the bold words that you're brave enough to say,
when you compliment a stranger on what they're wearing that day.
It dances down the aisle when you're walking on the bus,
and people move their legs aside so as not to cause a fuss.
You'll feel it when you're giving someone you love a cuddle,
and you'll see tiny glimmers of it
when you're going through a struggle.
It's hidden in the litter you choose to pick up off the floor,
and it floats through the air when you wait to hold the door.
It's the way when someone sneezes, you say, 'oh, bless you!'
when you wish someone a nice day
and they smile and wish you one too.
You see, it's not always the big things that make life worth living,
because the most magical thing of all is being kind and giving.

I'm in constant awe
of the courage you find.
Life has dealt you a cruel hand,
but still, you are so kind.
You make time for other people
and you love with your whole heart.
You are so beautifully held together,
when you could have been torn apart.
You truly are incredible,
I never want you to forget.
The world has been a much lovelier place,
since we first met.

When you see someone hurting,
don't look away.
It can't wait until later,
or until another day.
Even if it feels uncomfortable
for you to see their pain,
it takes seconds to offer an umbrella
to someone in the rain.
If we all took a few minutes
for a struggling stranger each day,
almost eight billion lives would be changed
in the simplest of ways.
You may think you're too busy
to stop and help for a while,
but it doesn't have to be enormous,
often it's as simple as a smile.
Next time you see someone hurting,
don't walk away, show that you care.
You don't ever have to be perfect,
it just matters that you're there.

I once saw a quote
that said I shouldn't cross the sea
for people who wouldn't even think about
doing the same for me.
I thought about it for a while
and I know just what those words mean;
it's so easy to get disheartened
when people aren't always what they seem.
But then I reconsidered.
because why shouldn't I be kind,
to everyone I meet,
and that's why I changed my mind.
Who am I to judge,
who most deserves my love and care?
Everyone has a story
and not every story is fair.
I don't want this world to make me bitter,
so I will get in my boat and cross the sea.
Because my kindness is not a reflection of them,
it is a reflection of me.

We are all born with a sparkle
that lights us up like magic,
but over the years we're taught to hide
and that is what's most tragic.
We're told to be quieter,
to dull our sparkle down.
Over time it fades
and we start to lose our crown.
You learn to take your sparkle
and put it in your pocket,
or leave it in the cupboard
and use a key to lock it.
Maybe it's time we stopped conforming
and used our sparkles to light the way
and then perhaps tomorrow
would be a much brighter day.

I want to live in each moment,
I want to stay there for a while
I don't want to forget a single detail,
not the familiar warmth of your smile,
or the lovely roar of your laughter
so unapologetic and bold,
I don't want this to ever become yesterday,
and fade away as I grow old.
I hope the way your eyes twinkle
will always be here, in my mind,
if I hold it tight enough, and carry it,
and never leave it behind.

When I first saw the storm brewing
from the corner of my eye,
I felt fear start to flood through me,
so I started to run and hide.
From my makeshift shelter,
I watched debris tumble down,
chaos tearing through the world,
fire ripping through my town.
But when the flames stopped roaring,
it became clear to me,
that the universe had placed me,
right where I needed to be.
It was then I accepted that sometimes
you have to bear the wrath,
because not all storms are vicious,
some come to clear your path.

There's something about rainbows,
that always soothes my soul.
They remind me of what the light is
when the sky is black as coal.
When the darkness overpowers me
and hope is nowhere to be seen,
a bridge of colour appears
where the pouring rain has been.
It's like the world is saying,
it's okay to live through storms.
There's always a trace of sunshine,
though it won't always be warm.
I know when the clouds start filling
and the sky turns a frightening grey,
no matter how loud the thunder is now,
the downpour never stays.
There will always be a rainbow,
and so there will always be hope.
I keep searching for those beautiful colours,
and that is how I cope.

Never stop looking up,
dreaming of bigger things,
of impossible adventures
and growing your wings.
Watching the clouds
as they slowly float past,
so graceful and constant,
when life moves too fast.
It's good to stay grounded,
but don't live solely on earth.
Keep your head in the clouds,
until you start to see your worth.

The evening seems to drown me
in a sea of fresh new dreams,
as I dance through rapeseed fields
and settle by a stream.
Somehow the flow of water
as it washes over me
reminds me that each droplet
will drain into the sea.
I lean against a tree trunk
and gaze into the woods;
this life isn't a puzzle
nor a story to be understood.
Life is complicated
but sitting here, right now,
everything seems so simple,
it's hard to imagine how.

The people looked with wonder
at the girl crouched on the ground.
She had gone to pick some flowers,
but there were no flowers to be found.
Instead, she was holding,
between two tightly closed fists,
a handful of freshly picked dandelions
that she intended as gifts.
They didn't need gift wrapping
or tying with a bow.
She looked down and saw their beauty
and wanted everyone to know.
So she carried them around
and handed them out to folk.
She held them like they were precious
but they all muttered and joked.
Her eyes were wide open with wonder,
even though she watched them resist.
All those people saw a pointless weed,
but that little girl saw a wish.

In order to fly,
you must first fall.
When you look at the big picture,
failure isn't scary at all.
One leap out into the open,
and then you'll grow your wings.
Surely stumbling is okay,
in the grand scheme of things.

Stop waiting for the weekend,
for your holiday, for tonight.
When you wish away the seconds,
it's so easy to lose sight
of all those tiny moments
that pass us by each day
we're so busy looking to the future,
but those moments never stay
still enough to capture with a camera
and a smile
so maybe we should stop in our tracks
and just breathe every once in a while.
Notice those things around you
that slip past without a trace;
the smell of rain, a soft fresh breeze,
the freckles on your face,
the stars at night, a flower that grows
through cracks in the pavement on the street,
hearing someone laugh, the ocean's roar
and all of the food you eat.
Breathe, and take a minute,
to stand still and just stay.
Stop waiting for the next moment,
because life is happening today.

Slowly I am learning
to appreciate each day.
Even if it broke my heart,
it was special in a way,
for every day becomes a piece
in a massive picture frame,
even the boring, aching days,
and it would be a shame
to let even a second slip by
without acknowledging it first.
I am slowly understanding
how to see each day's own worth,
because those tiny fleeting moments
are the bricks that build our past.
It's so sad we often miss them
as they fly by much too fast.

Because time moves so quickly,
it's sometimes hard to see,
that you're moving far away
from the person you used to be.
Now there is a bed of wildflowers
where darkness used to stay,
and the pain that you used to carry,
the ocean has washed away.
You don't always notice it,
but you're changing a little each day.
You're not following the same path any more,
you're growing your own way.

I got tired of waiting
for the sun to find me.
I couldn't spend my days waiting,
I had too much to see.
So one day I woke up
and decided to change.
It didn't happen overnight
and at first it seemed strange.
I had to start walking
and leave the past behind
but I had to move quickly
in case I changed my mind.
I dug up my roots
and planted them somewhere new.
I waited and waited
and finally, I grew.
I started to bloom
as the sun began to shine.
and my growth wasn't perfect
but at least it was mine.

These days I'm getting better
at letting people go.
No matter how much it hurts me,
it's what I have to do to grow.
The people who are toxic,
who drain the life from me,
those who use and manipulate
and it's taken me so long to see
that I'm better off without them
and I'm whole all on my own.
I may not have crowds of people
but I'll never be alone.

There were moments you thought
you wouldn't make it this far.
You wanted to give up,
and yet, here you are.
There were days your hands trembled
and your voice shook with fear.
People trampled your spirits,
but still, you made it here.
Take a second to marvel
at how incredible you really are.
It's easy to forget,
that you have come so far.

It is important to me
to sometimes feel small,
to be reminded that my troubles
aren't really that big at all,
to be surrounded by rolling hills,
a scene a thousand times my size,
to walk through forests much older than I am,
to touch the bark of trees, ancient and wise.
There is something so reassuring,
in that the incredible world I see
was here long before I was,
and will be here long after me.
If something seems enormous,
it never feels it sat up here.
I just look out across the ocean,
and my problems disappear.

Once there was a time
when I thought that walking away
was the weakest thing to do,
and so I would always stay
in places I didn't fit,
doing things not meant for me,
but after years of staying,
I cut my ties and broke free.
I turned and walked away
and I didn't stop for miles.
Walking away didn't come naturally
and the journey took a while.
Sometimes I had to walk in darkness,
without a map, alone,
but somehow, I always found my way,
that's how I know I've grown,
and now my shoes are well weathered,
from all the walking I've done.
I don't mind the walking any more,
I keep searching for the sun.

I'm unapologetic these days,
because I don't want to live with fear,
or fade into the background
and simply disappear.
I don't want to be afraid
of doing the things I adore,
to wake up with regrets,
left always wanting more.
I want to live my life with passion,
unafraid to be silly and bold.
If I make mistakes then so be it,
I'll have stories to tell when I'm old.
And now I'm finally finding
the person I've always wanted to be;
life is too short to being anything but
unapologetically me.

The days you wake up to now
are fresh and new.
You watch the future unfold,
after the things you've lived through.
The pain brought you to this moment,
though it doesn't make it right.
You are starting to see glimmers
of a future that once wasn't in sight.
Life still isn't perfect,
and sometimes it's one big storm,
but at least you're more prepared now
to keep yourself warm.
Look out through your window,
your path has been cleared.
There is an air of excitement
in the days you once feared.
You can walk away the past,
the places you've come from.
You'll leave your house and find the sunshine,
and you'll be so glad you held on.

Printed in Great Britain
by Amazon

65117324R00026